Genre **Expository Text**

Essential Question
How do people make government work?

The Race for the Presidency

by Mary Atkinson

Introduction	2
Chapter 1 The Primary Election	4
Chapter 2 The General Election	8
Chapter 3 Election Day	12
Respond to Reading	15
PAIRED READ Elementary School Lawmakers	16
Focus on Social Studies	19

Introduction

Have you ever **voted** for a class president? Classmates who want to be class president are the **candidates**.

The candidates give speeches. They say what they will do if they win. Students vote for the person they think will be the best president. The candidate with the most votes wins.

Kelly Ca was a class president. She gave a speech in 2010. She spoke for President Obama.

The elections for President of the United States are like a class election. But they are held every four years. The election race takes more than a year.

The President must be at least 35 years old. Theodore Roosevelt became President at age 42.

Chapter 1
The Primary Election

The race for the Presidency starts with primary elections. Most candidates belong to a political party. There are two main parties: Democrats and Republicans. Voters from each party choose candidates.

Some candidates are **independent**. They don't belong to a party.

Most states have a primary election. Each main party picks a candidate.

Democratic candidate Hillary Clinton ran for president in 2008 and 2016. Here she talks with voters in 2008.

The candidates in a primary election meet voters. They give speeches. The candidates say what they would do if voters **elect** them.

Voters vote at a polling place.

Next, the two main parties hold meetings. The meetings are called **conventions**. They **announce** their candidates. The parties then plan **campaigns**.

> **STOP AND CHECK**
> What are primary elections?

The winning candidates for president and vice president are chosen at conventions.

Chapter 2
The General Election

The campaigns to become President begin. The candidates travel around the country. They meet with voters. Many people work hard for each campaign. They plan events. They raise money.

George W. Bush meets with supporters during his 2000 campaign for president.

Candidates ask what kind of **government** people want. They talk to people. They find out about any problems. The candidates **collect** the answers.

Trains carried candidates in the past. They made "whistle-stop tours."

Candidates have debates. They discuss their plans. Candidates make promises. Reporters ask the candidates questions.

Hillary Clinton and Donald Trump held debates before the 2016 election so voters could hear their ideas.

Republican candidate Richard M. Nixon (left) and Democratic candidate John F. Kennedy in a debate on TV in 1960

The debates are on TV. Voters want to know if a candidate's ideas will work. Debates help voters make **decisions** about how to vote.

STOP AND CHECK

What do candidates do during a debate?

Chapter 3
Election Day

Election Day is on the first Tuesday in November. People vote at polling places.

Today, most people 18 and over can vote. It wasn't always like this. People have had to work hard for the right to vote.

Women marched in 1920. They wanted voting rights.

Election Day is exciting. Who will win? People **estimate** who will get the most votes. The winners are announced.

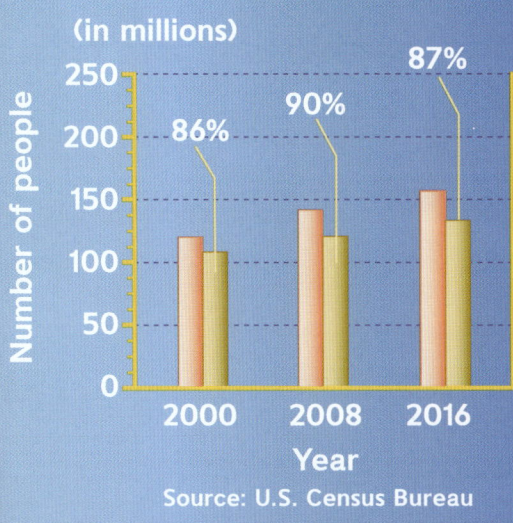

Voting in Presidential Elections

- People who registered to vote
- People who voted

Source: U.S. Census Bureau

A graph showing how many people voted in three different elections

The President is sworn in on January 20. This is Inauguration Day. The **ceremony** is in Washington, D.C. The President's **term** in office begins.

Barack Obama in 2009 starting his term as the 44th President of the United States

STOP AND CHECK

What happens on Election Day?

Respond to Reading

Summarize

Summarize the information in this book. You may use the chart to help you.

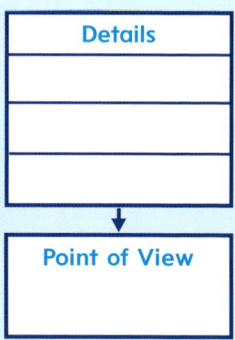

Text Evidence

1. Reread page 13. What is the author's point of view about Election Day? **Author's Point of View**

2. Find the word *debates* on page 10. What does it mean? What clues helped you? **Vocabulary**

3. Write about why the author thinks the candidate debates are important. Use details from the text in your answer. **Write About Reading**

Genre Expository Text

Compare Texts
Read about how students changed a law.

Elementary School Lawmakers

Some New Hampshire students wanted to change a law in 2006. They wanted the pumpkin to be the state fruit. Pumpkins grow throughout the state.

Pumpkins stacked up on display at a festival in Keene, New Hampshire

Peter Allen was a state representative. He liked the students' idea. He gave a bill to the House. He asked that the pumpkin become the state fruit.

The students asked other students for support. They wrote postcards. The bill was passed in the House. Then it needed to pass in the Senate.

A pumpkin is a fruit. It contains seeds.

The senators voted. The pumpkin was voted in! The students had become lawmakers.

NEW HAMPSHIRE LAW

CHAPTER 3: STATE EMBLEMS, FLAG, ETC.

Section 3:24 State Fruit.
3:24 State Fruit. – The pumpkin is hereby designated as the official state fruit of New Hampshire.

Make Connections

Do people know what the result will be when they vote for a bill? **Essential Question**

What do candidates do to get votes? How did the students do the same to get people to vote for the pumpkin? **Text to Text**

Focus on Social Studies

Purpose To see how surveys can be used for campaigning

What to Do

Step 1 Make a list of colors (or some other item). Ask each person to choose their favorite.

Step 2 Write the number of people who chose each item.

Step 3 Make a "Vote for..." poster for the second most popular item.

Step 4 Have a vote between the first and second most popular items.

Conclusion Which item did you think would be the most popular? How did your ideas change?